ÂF198989

Impressum
Verlag: BABADADA GmbH, Nedderfeld 112 , 22529 Hamburg
Geschäftsführer / Verlagsleitung: Harald Hof
Druck: Books on Demand GmbH, In de Tarpen 42, 22848 Norderstedt

Imprint
Publisher: BABADADA GmbH, Nedderfeld 112 , 22529 Hamburg, Germany
Managing Director / Publishing direction: Harald Hof
Print: Books on Demand GmbH, In de Tarpen 42, 22848 Norderstedt

school
School

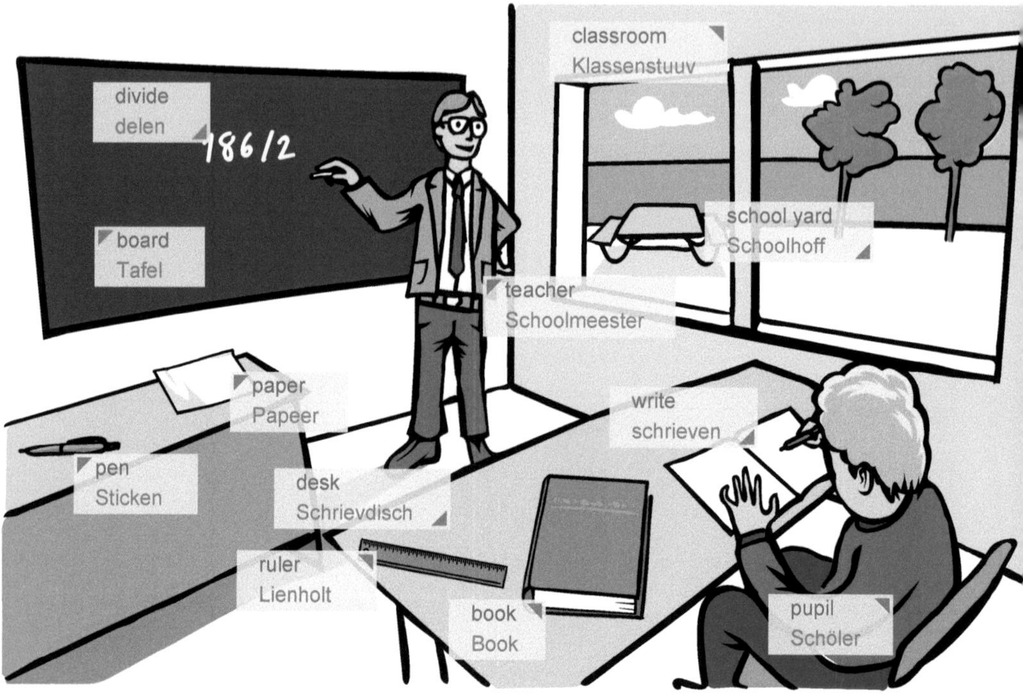

classroom
Klassenstuuv
divide
delen
186/2
board
Tafel
school yard
Schoolhoff
teacher
Schoolmeester
paper
Papeer
write
schrieven
pen
Sticken
desk
Schrievdisch
ruler
Lienholt
book
Book
pupil
Schöler

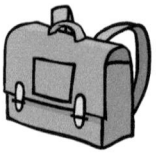

satchel

Ranzel

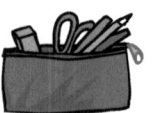

pencil case

Feddermapp

pencil

Bleesticken

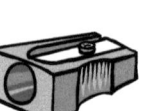

pencil sharpener

Scharpmaker

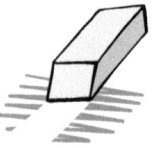

rubber

Radeergummi

drawing pad

Tekenblock

drawing
Teken

paintbrush
Pinsel

paint box
Malkassen

scissors
Scheer

glue
Klever

exercise book
Heft to'n Öven

homework
Huusopgaav

number
Tall

add
tohooptellen

subtract
aftrecken

multiply
malnehmen

calculate
reken

letter
Bookstaav

alphabet
ABC

word
Woort

text
Text

read
lesen

chalk
Kried

lesson
Stunn

register
Klassenbook

exam
Pröven

certificate
Tüügnis

school uniform
Schooluniform

education
Utbillen

encyclopedia
Nakieksel

university
Universität

microscope
Mikroskop

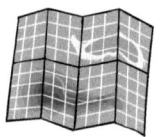

map
Koort

waste-paper basket
Papeerkorf

travel
Törn

hotel
Hotel
Grand
hostel
Harbarg
ROOMS
bureau de change
Wesselstuuv
car
Auto

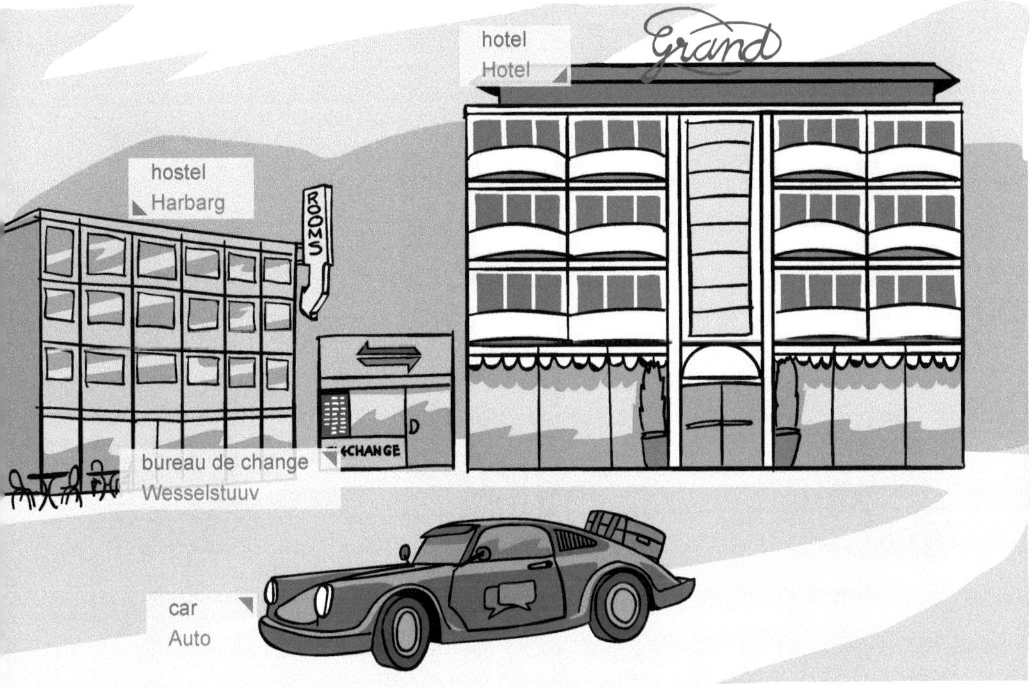

language

Spraak

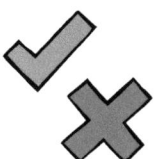

yes / no

jo / ne

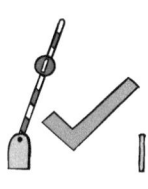

Okay

Jo

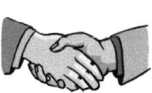

hello

Moin

translator

Översetter

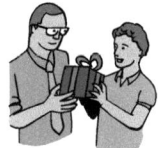

Thank you

Dank ok

how much is...?

Wat kost...?

I do not understand

Ik verstah nich

problem

Problem

Good evening!

Goden Avend

Good morning!

Moin!

Good night!

Gode Nacht!

bye bye

Tschüüs

direction

Richt

luggage

Bagaasch

bag

Tasch

backpack

Rüchsack

guest

Gast

room

Stuuv

sleeping bag

Slaapsack

tent

Telt

tourist information

Touristeninformatschoon

beach

Strand

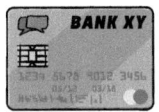

credit card

Kreditkoort

breakfast

Fröhstück

lunch

Meddageten

dinner

Avendeten

ticket

Fohrkort

lift

Fohrstohl

stamp

Breefmark

border

Grenz

customs

Toll

embassy

Bottschop

visa

Visum

passport

Pass

transport
Transport

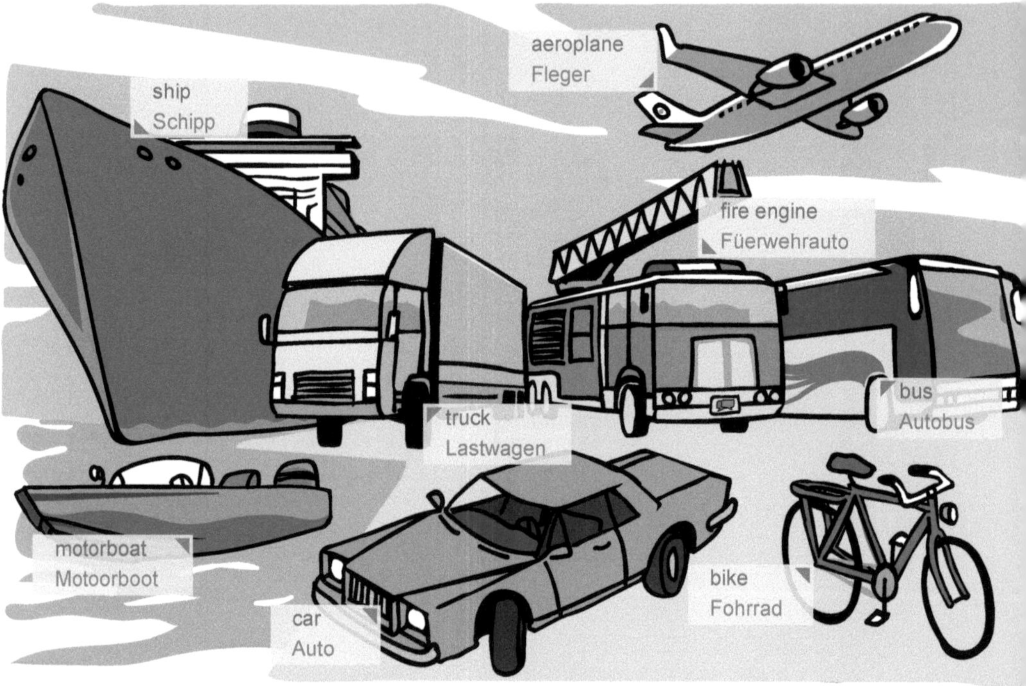

ship
Schipp
aeroplane
Fleger
fire engine
Füerwehrauto
truck
Lastwagen
bus
Autobus
motorboat
Motoorboot
car
Auto
bike
Fohrrad

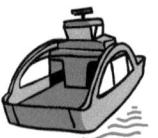

ferry

Fähr

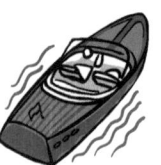

boat

Boot

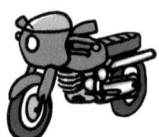

motorbike

Motoorrad

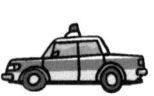

police car

Polizeiauto

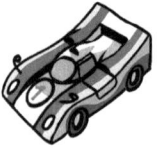

racing car

Rönnauto

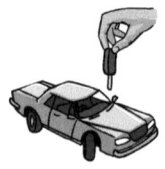

rental car

Lehnwagen

car sharing

Carsharing

breakdown truck

Afsleepwagen

refuse truck

Müllauto

motor

Motoor

fuel

Kraftstoff

petrol station

Tanksteed

traffic sign

Verkehrsschild

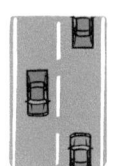

traffic

Verkehr

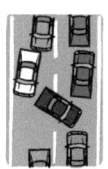

traffic jam

Stau

car park

Afstellplatz

train station

Bahnhoff

tracks

Sporen

train

Tog

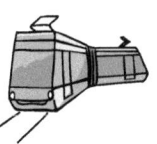

tram

Stratenbahn

carriage

Wagon

helicopter

Dwarsmöhl

airport

Flooghaven

tower

Tower

passenger

Fohrgast

container

Grootkist

carton

Karton

cart

Koor

basket

Korf

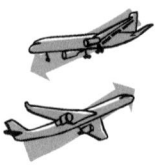

take off / land

starten / lannen

city

Stadt

village

Dörp

city centre

Binnenstadt

house

Huus

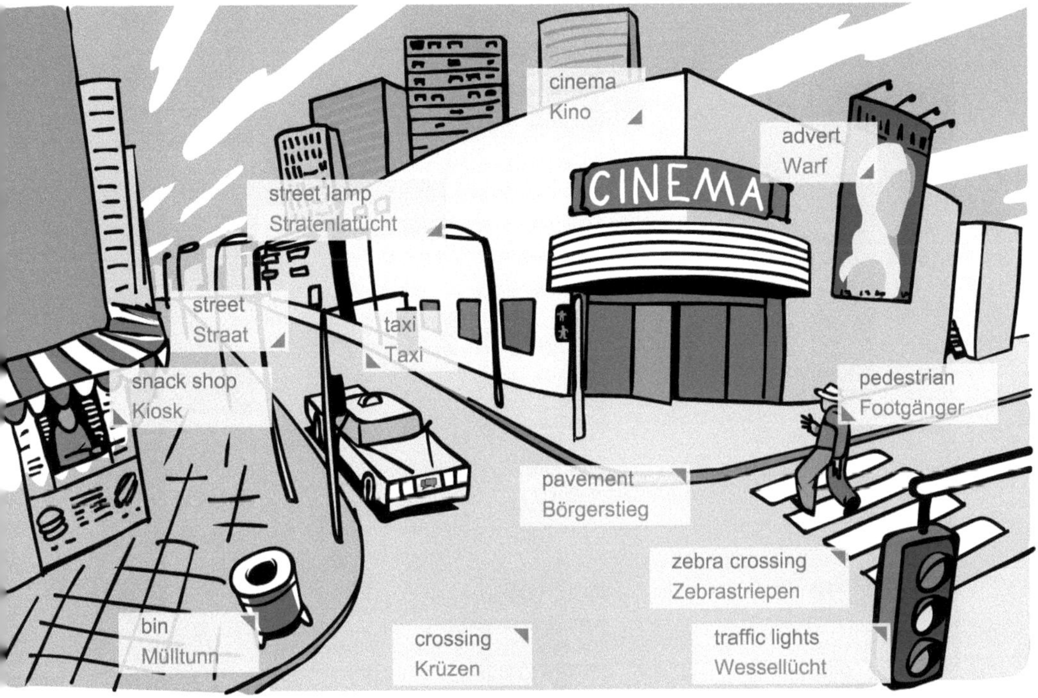

cinema
Kino

advert
Warf

street lamp
Stratenlatücht

CINEMA

street
Straat

taxi
Taxi

snack shop
Kiosk

pedestrian
Footgänger

pavement
Börgerstieg

zebra crossing
Zebrastriepen

bin
Mülltunn

crossing
Krüzen

traffic lights
Wessellücht

hut

Hütt

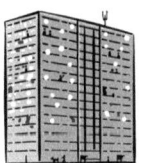

flat

Wahnung

train station

Bahnhoff

town hall

Raathuus

museum

Museum

school

School

university
Universität

bank
Bank

hospital
Krankenhuus

hotel
Hotel

pharmacy
Afteek

office
Büro

book shop
Bookhökerie

shop
Hökerie

florist's
Blomenhökerie

supermarket
Supermarkt

market
Markt

department store
Koophuus

fishmonger's
Fischhökerie

shopping centre
Inkoopszentrum

harbour
Haven

park

Parkanlaag

bench

Bank

bridge

Brüch

stairs

Trepp

underground

Ünnergrundbahn

tunnel

Tunnel

bus stop

Busstoppsteed

bar

Bar

restaurant

Spieslokal

postbox

Breefkassen

street sign

Stratenschild

parking meter

Parkklock

zoo

Deertenpark

swimming pool

Baadanstalt

mosque

Moschee

farm
Buernhoff

pollution
Ümweltversmudden

graveyard
Karkhoff

church
Kark

playground
Speelplatz

temple
Tempel

landscape
Landschop

signpost
Wiespahl

way
Weg

meadow
Wisch

stone
Steen

tree
Boom

hiker
Wannerer

river
Fluss

grass
Gras

flower
Bloom

valley

Daal

hill

Barg

lake

See

forest

Holt

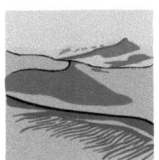

desert

Wööst

volcano

Füerspien Barg

castle

Slott

rainbow

Regenbagen

mushroom

Poggenstohl

palm tree

Palm

mosquito

Steekmück

fly

Fleeg

ant

Miegeemk

bee

Imm

spider

Spinn

beetle
Sebber

frog
Pogg

squirrel
Katteker

hedgehog
Swienegel

hare
Haas

owl
Uul

bird
Vagel

swan
Swaan

boar
Wildswien

deer
Hirsch

moose
Elk

dam
Staudamm

wind turbine
Windrad

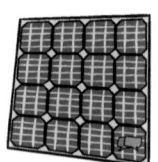

solar panel
Solarmodul

climate
Klima

restaurant
Spieslokal

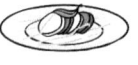

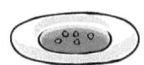

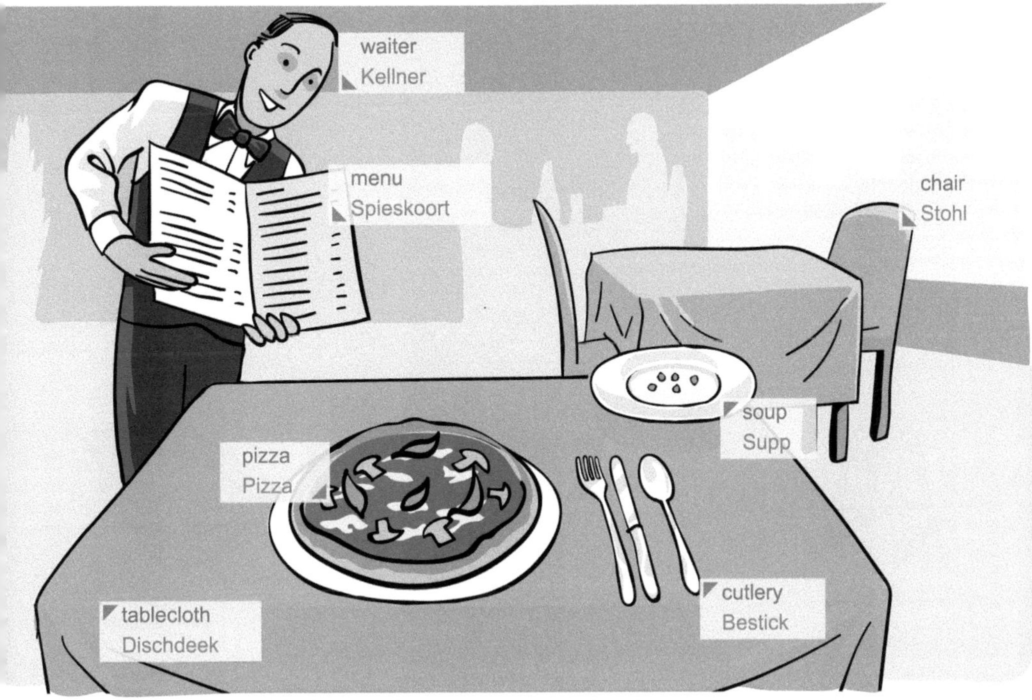
waiter
Kellner
menu
Spieskoort
chair
Stohl
soup
Supp
pizza
Pizza
tablecloth
Dischdeek
cutlery
Bestick

starter

Vörspies

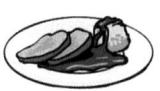

main course

Haupteten

dessert

Nadisch

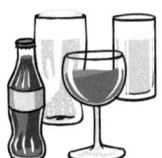

drinks

Drünk

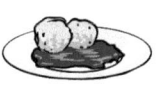

food

Eten

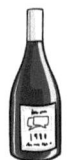

bottle

Buddel

fast food

Fastfood

street food

Strateneten

teapot

Teekann

sugar bowl

Zuckerdoos

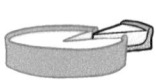

portion

Portschoon

espresso machine

Espressomaschien

high chair

Hoochstohl

bill

Reken

tray

Tablett

knife

Mess

fork

Gavel

spoon

Lepel

teaspoon

Teelepel

serviette

Munddook

glass

Glas

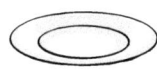

plate

Töller

soup plate

Suppentöller

saucer

Ünnertass

sauce

Sooß

salt pot

Soltstreuer

pepper mill

Pepermöhl

vinegar

Etig

oil

Ööl

spices

Krüder

ketchup

Ketchup

mustard

Mostrich

mayonnaise

Mayonnaise

supermarket
Supermarkt

special offer
Anbott
customer
Kunn
FOR
dairy
Melkprodukten
trolley
Inkoopswagen
fruit
Aaft

BUTCHERS

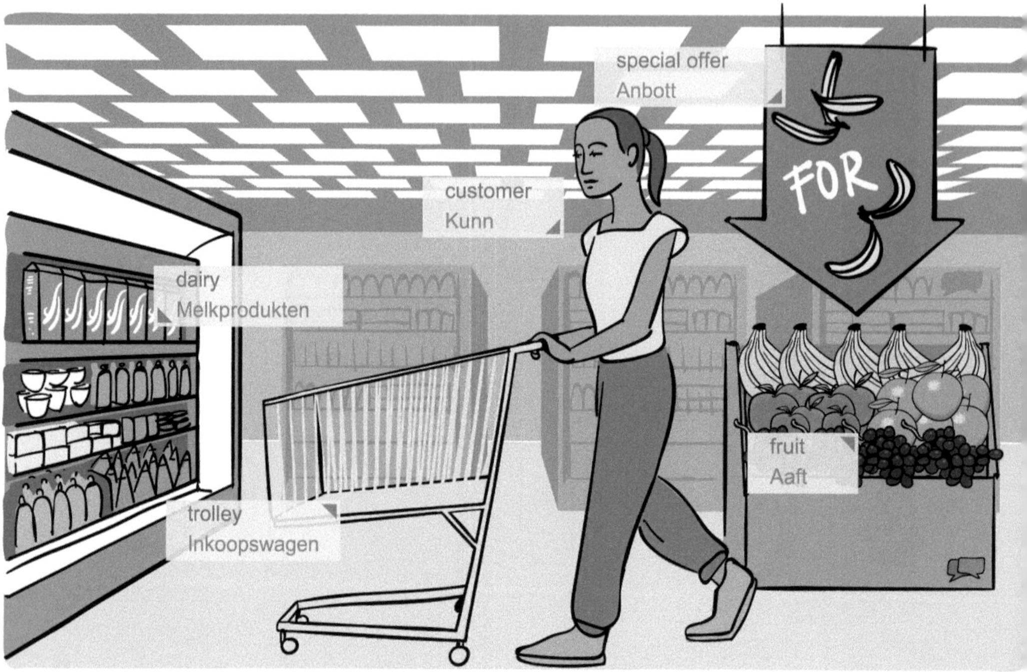

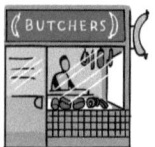

butcher´s
Slachterie

BAKERY

baker´s
Bäckerie

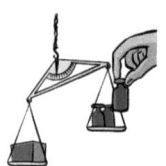

weigh
wegen

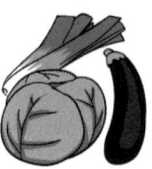

vegetables
Gröönsaken

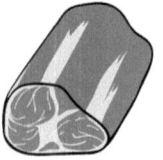

meat
Fleesch

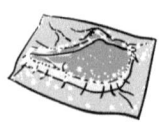

frozen food
Deepköhlkost

cold meat

Opsnitt

tinned food

Konserven

washing powder

Waschmiddel

sweets

Snoopkraam

household products

Huushooltssaken

cleaning products

Reinmaaktüüch

salesperson

Verköpersche

till

Kass

cashier

Kasserer

shopping list

Inkoopslist

opening hours

Opsparrtieden

wallet

Breeftasch

credit card

Kreditkoort

bag

Tasch

plastic bag

Plastiktüüt

water

Water

juice

Saft

milk

Melk

coke

Cola

wine

Wien

beer

Beer

alcohol

Spriet

cocoa

Kakao

tea

Tee

coffee

Koffie

espresso

Espresso

cappuccino

Cappucino

banana

Banaan

apple

Appel

orange

Appelsien

melon

Meloon

lemon

Zitroon

carrot

Wöttel

garlic

Knuuvlook

bamboo

Bambus

onion

Zibbel

mushroom

Poggenstohl

nuts

Nööt

noodles

Nudeln

spaghetti

Spaghetti

rice

Ries

salad

Salat

chips

Pommes frites

fried potatoes

Braadkantüffeln

pizza

Pizza

hamburger

Hamborger

sandwich

Sandwich

cutlet

Snitzel

ham

Schinken

salami

Salami

sausage

Wust

chicken

Hohn

roast

Braden

fish

Fisch

porridge oats

Haverflocken

muesli

Müsli

cornflakes

Cornflakes

flour

Mehl

croissant

Croissant

bread roll

Rundstück

bread

Broot

toast

Toast

biscuits

Keksen

butter

Botter

curd

Quark

cake

Koken

egg

Ei

fried egg

Spegelei

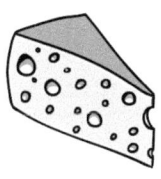

cheese

Kees

ice cream

les

sugar

Zucker

honey

Honnig

jam

Marmelaad

chocolate spread

Nougat-Creme

curry

Curry

farm
Buernhoff

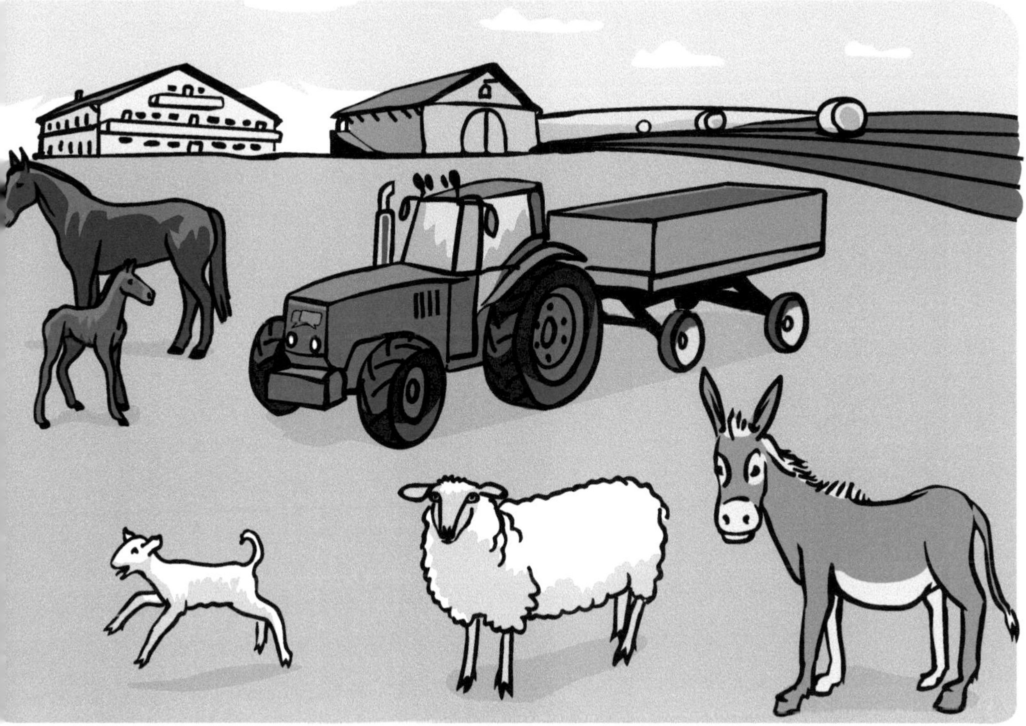

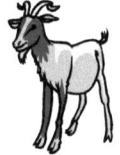

goat

Zeeg

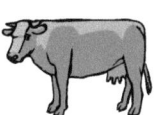

cow

Koh

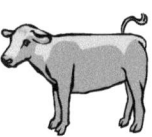

calf

Kalf

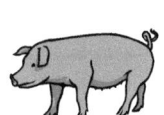

pig

Swien

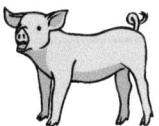

piglet

Farken

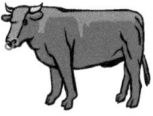

bull

Bull

goose

Goos

duck

Aant

chick

Küken

hen

Hohn

cock

Hahn

rat

Rott

cat

Katt

mouse

Muus

ox

Oss

dog

Hund

doghouse

Hunnenhütt

garden hose

Goornslauch

watering can

Geetkann

scythe

Lee

plough

Ploog

sickle

Sich

hoe

Hack

pitchfork

Mestfork

axe

Ext

wheelbarrow

Schuufkoor

trough

Trog

milk can

Melkkann

sack

Sack

fence

Tuun

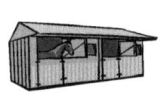

stable

Stall

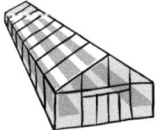

greenhouse

Drievhuus

soil

Bodden

seed

Saat

fertilizer

Dünger

combine harvester

Meihdöscher

harvest

oornen

harvest

Oorn

yams

Yamswöttel

wheat

Weten

soy

Soja

potato

Kantüffel

corn

Törksche Weten

rapeseed

Rapp

fruit tree

Aaftboom

cassava

Troopsch Kantüffel

cereals

Koorn

house
Huus

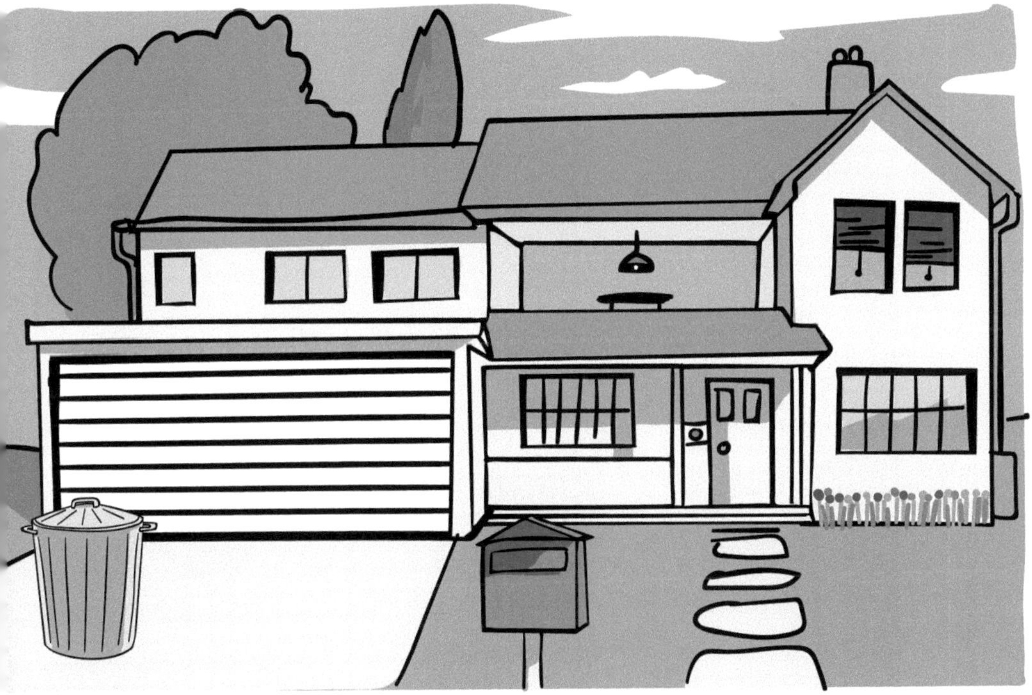

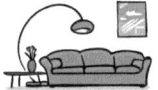

living room

Wahnstuuv

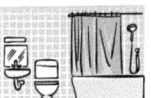

bathroom

Baadstuuv

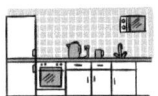

kitchen

Köök

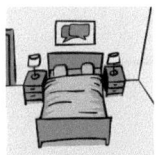

bedroom

Slaapstuuv

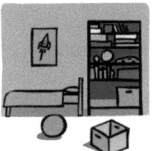

child's room

Kinnerstuuv

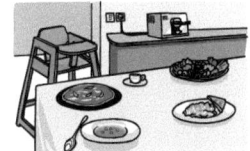

dining room

Eetstuuv

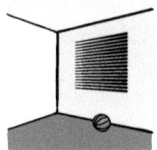

floor

Footbodden

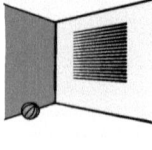

wall

Wand

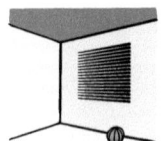

ceiling

Deek

cellar

Keller

sauna

Hittluftbad

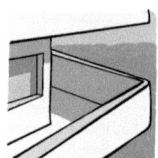

balcony

Balkon

terrace

Terrass

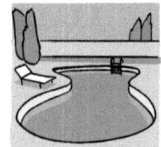

pool

Swümmbad

lawn mower

Rasenmeiher

sheet

Bettbetog

bedspread

Bettdeek

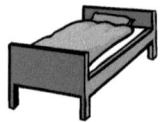

bed

Puuch

broom

Bessen

bucket

Emmer

switch

Schalter

living room
Wahnstuuv

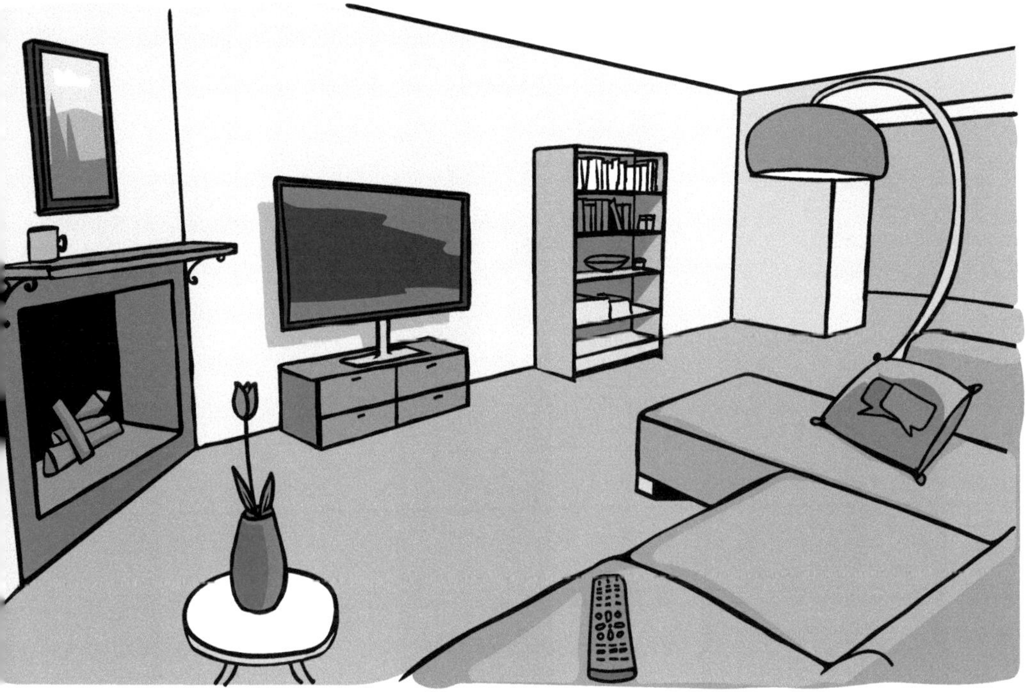

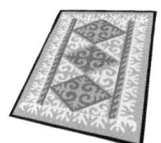

carpet

Teppich

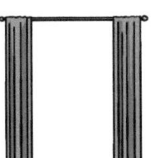

curtain

Vörhang

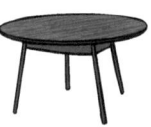

table

Disch

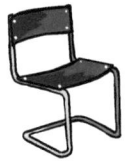

chair

Stohl

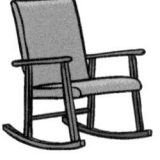

rocking chair

Schuckelstohl

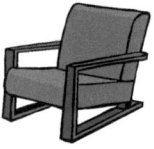

armchair

Sessel

book

Book

blanket

Deek

decoration

Dekoratschoon

firewood

Füerholt

film

Film

hi-fi equipment

Stereoanlaag

key

Slötel

newspaper

Narichtenblatt

painting

Gemälde

poster

Poster

radio

Radio

notepad

Opschrievblock

hoover

Huulbessen

cactus

Kaktus

candle

Kars

kitchen
Köök

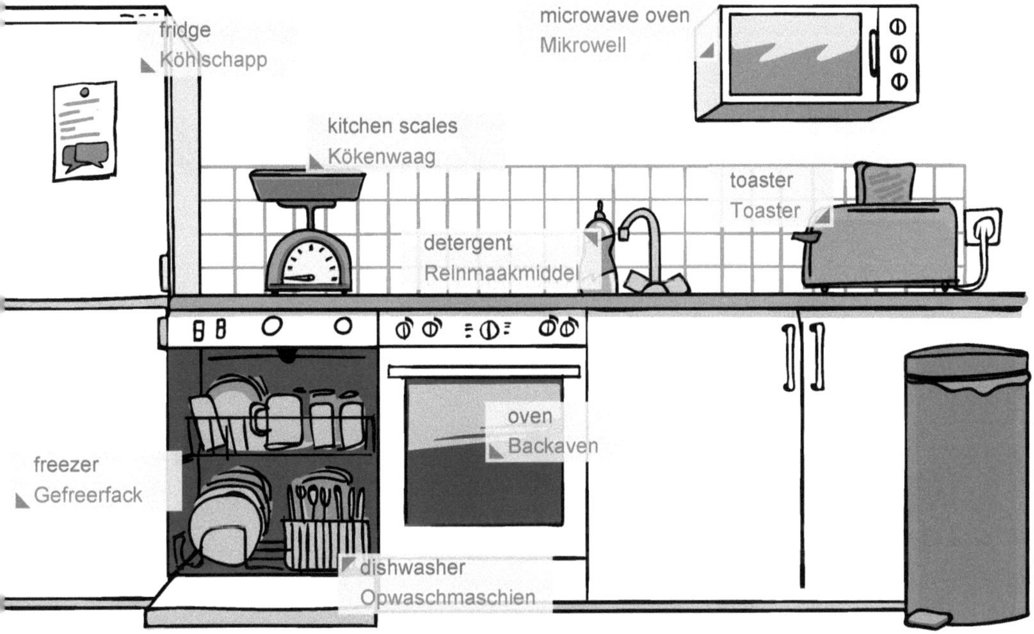

fridge
Köhlschapp
microwave oven
Mikrowell
kitchen scales
Kökenwaag
toaster
Toaster
detergent
Reinmaakmiddel
oven
Backaven
freezer
Gefreerfack
dishwasher
Opwaschmaschien

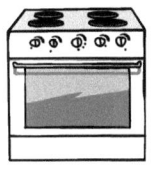

cooker
Heerd

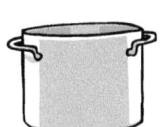

pot
Pott

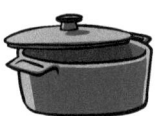

cast-iron pot
Gussiesern Putt

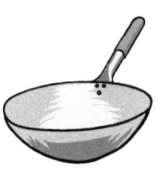

wok / kadai
Wok / Kadai

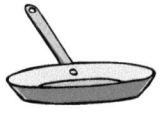

pan
Pann

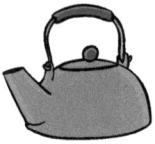

kettle
Waterkaker

steamer

Dampkaakputt

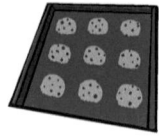

baking tray

Backblick

crockery

Geschirr

mug

Beker

bowl

Schaal

chopsticks

Eetsticken

ladle

Suppenkell

spatula

Pannenwenner

whisk

Sneebessen

strainer

Kaakseef

sieve

Seef

grater

Riev

mortar

Mörser

barbecue

Grill

open fire

Füerstell

chopping board
Sniedbrett

rolling pin
Nudelholt

corkscrew
Proppentrecker

can
Doos

can opener
Dosenaapner

pot holder
Pottlappen

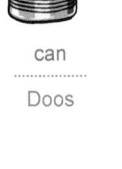

sink
Waschbecken

brush
Böst

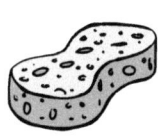

sponge
Swamm

blender
Mixer

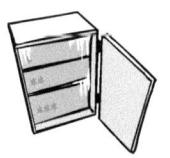

deep freezer
Iesschapp

baby bottle
Nuckelbuddel

tap
Waterhahn

bathroom
Baadstuuv

shower
Bruus
heating
Heizung
towel
Handdook
shower curtain
Bruusvörhang
bubble bath
Schuumbad
bathtub
Baadwann
glass
Glas
washing machine
Waschmaschien
tap
Waterhahn
tiles
Fliesen
potty
lütte Putt
sink
Waschbecken

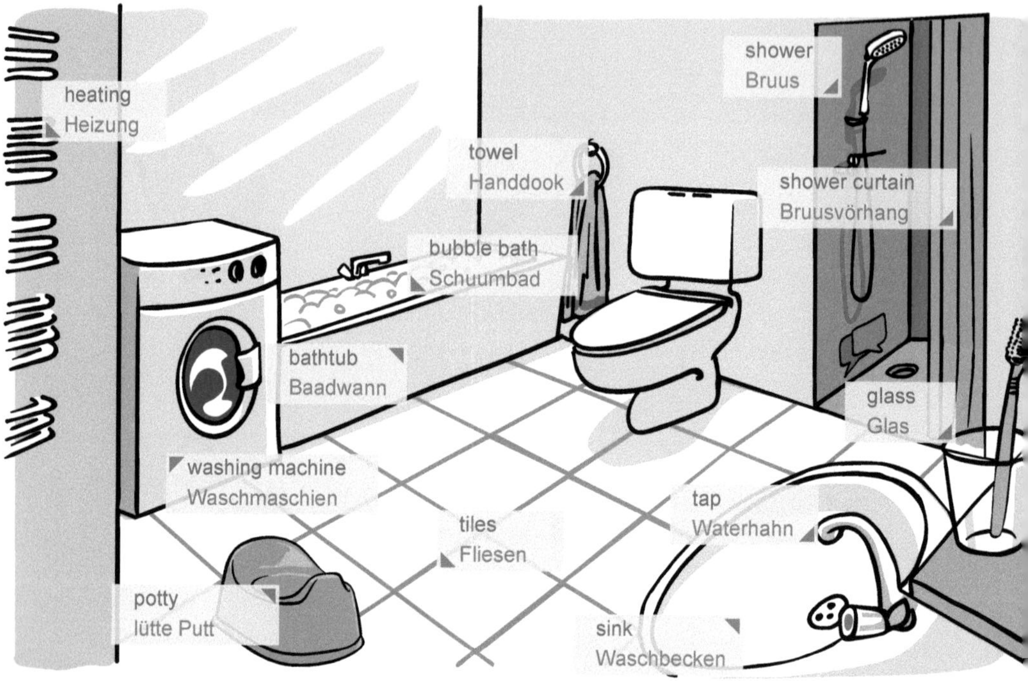

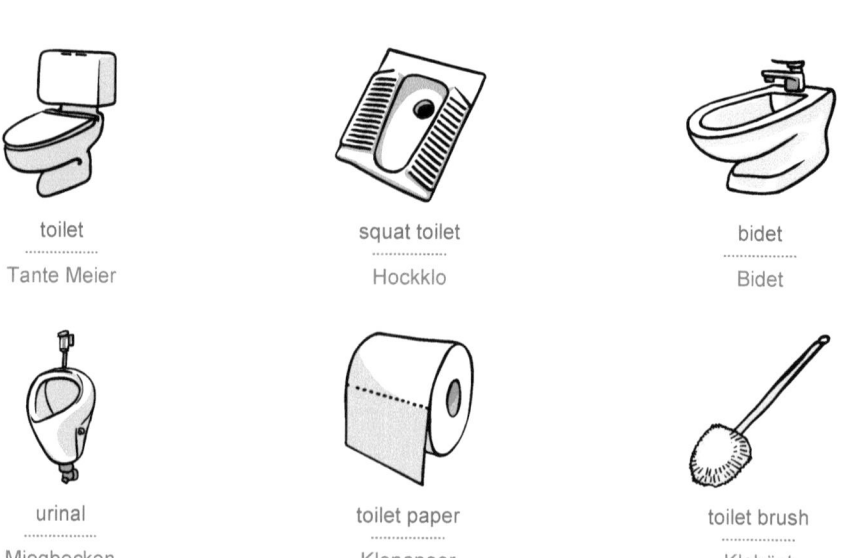

toilet
Tante Meier

squat toilet
Hockklo

bidet
Bidet

urinal
Miegbecken

toilet paper
Klopapeer

toilet brush
Klobőst

toothbrush

Tähnböst

toothpaste

Tähnpast

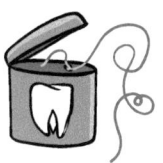

dental floss

Tähnsied

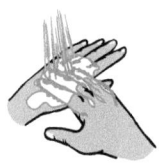

wash

waschen

handheld shower

Handbruus

douche

Intimbruus

basin

Waschschöttel

back brush

Rüchböst

soap

Seep

shower gel

Bruusgeel

shampoo

Hoorwaschmiddel

flannel

Waschlappen

drain

Afloop

cream

Creme

deodorant

Deodorant

mirror

Spegel

hand mirror

Kosmetikspegel

razor

Raserer

shaving foam

Raseerschuum

aftershave

Raseerwater

comb

Kamm

brush

Böst

hair dryer

Hoordröger

hairspray

Hoorspray

makeup

Smink

lipstick

Lippensticken

nail varnish

Nagellack

cotton wool

Watt

nail scissors

Nagelscheer

perfume

Rüükwater

washbag

Kulturbüdel

stool

Schemel

weighing scale

Waag

bathrobe

Baadmantel

rubber gloves

Gummihanschen

tampon

Tampon

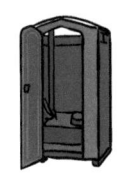

sanitary towel

Damenbinn

chemical toilet

Chemieklo

child's room

Kinnerstuuv

alarm clock
Wecker
cuddly toy
Knudeldeert
toy car
Speeltüüchauto
rattle
Klöter
doll's house
Poppenhuus
present
Geschenk

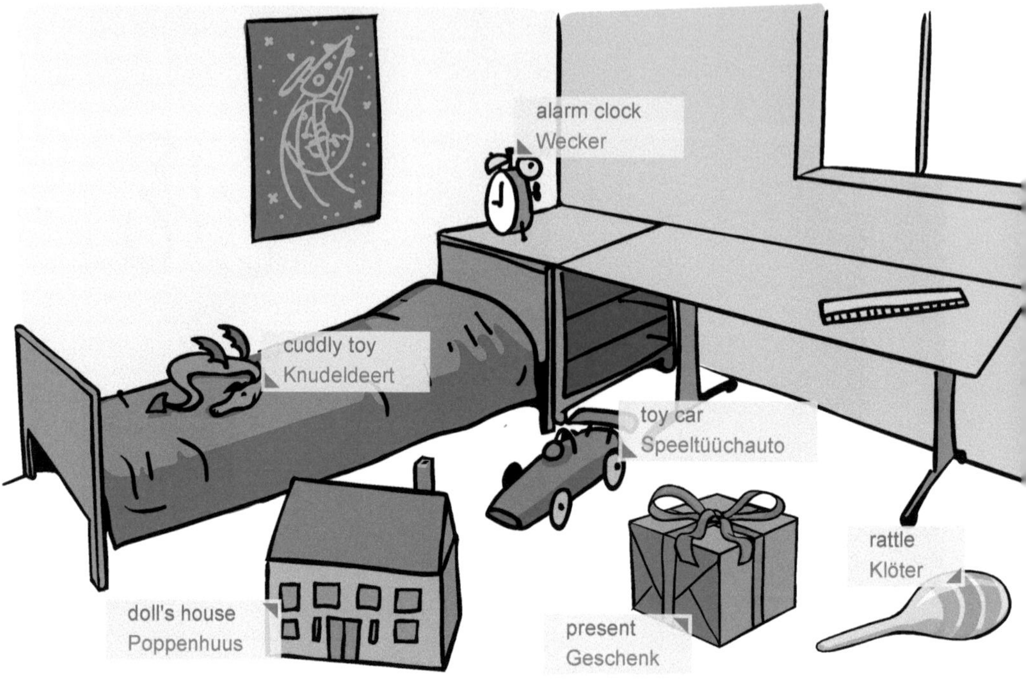

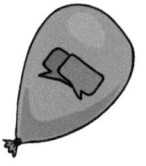

balloon

Luftballon

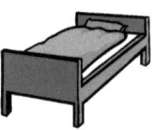

bed

Puuch

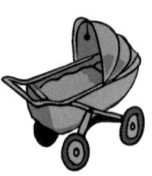

pram

Kinnerwagen

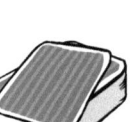

deck of cards

Koortenspeel

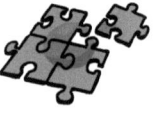

jigsaw

Puzzle

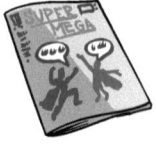

comic

Billergeschicht

lego bricks

Legostenen

building blocks

Bustenen

action figure

Action-Figur

babygrow

Strampelantog

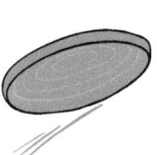

frisbee

Frisbeeschiev

mobile

Mobile

board game

Brettspeel

dice

Wörpel

model train set

Modelliesenbahn

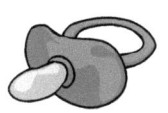

dummy

Snuller

party

Party

picture book

Billerbook

ball

Ball

doll

Popp

play

spelen

sandpit

Sandkassen

swing

Schuckel

toys

Speeltüüch

video game console

Speelkonsool

tricycle

Dreerad

teddy bear

Teddyboor

wardrobe

Klederschapp

clothing

Tüüch

socks

Socken

stockings

Strümp

tights

Strumpbüx

scarf
Halsdook

belt
Liefreem

umbrella
Paraplü

t-shirt
T-Shirt

trainers
Turnschoh

boots
Stevel

slippers
Puuschen

sandals
Sandalen

shoes
Schoh

rubber boots
Gummistevel

underpants
Ünnerbüx

bra
Bostholler

vest
Ünnerhemd

body
Lief

trousers
Büx

jeans
Jeansnüx

skirt
Rock

blouse
Bluus

shirt
Hemd

pullover
Pullover

hoodie
Kapuzenpullover

blazer
Blazer

jacket
Jack

coat
Mantel

raincoat
Övertrecker

costume
Kostüm

dress
Kleed

wedding dress
Hochtietskleed

suit

Antog

nightgown

Nachtkleed

pyjamas

Slaapantog

sari

Sari

headscarf

Koppdook

turban

Turban

burqa

Burka

kaftan

Kaftan

abaya

Abaya

swimsuit

Baadantog

trunks

Baadbüx

shorts

Korte Büx

tracksuit

Antog to'n Öven

apron

Schört

gloves

Handschoh

button

Knopp

glasses

Brill

bracelet

Armband

necklace

Halskeed

ring

Ring

earring

Ohrbummel

cap

Mütz

coat hanger

Klederbögel

hat

Hoot

tie

Binner

zip

Rietslüter

helmet

Helm

braces

Drachtband

school uniform

Schooluniform

uniform

Uniform

bib

Severböten

dummy

Snuller

nappy

Winnel

office

Büro

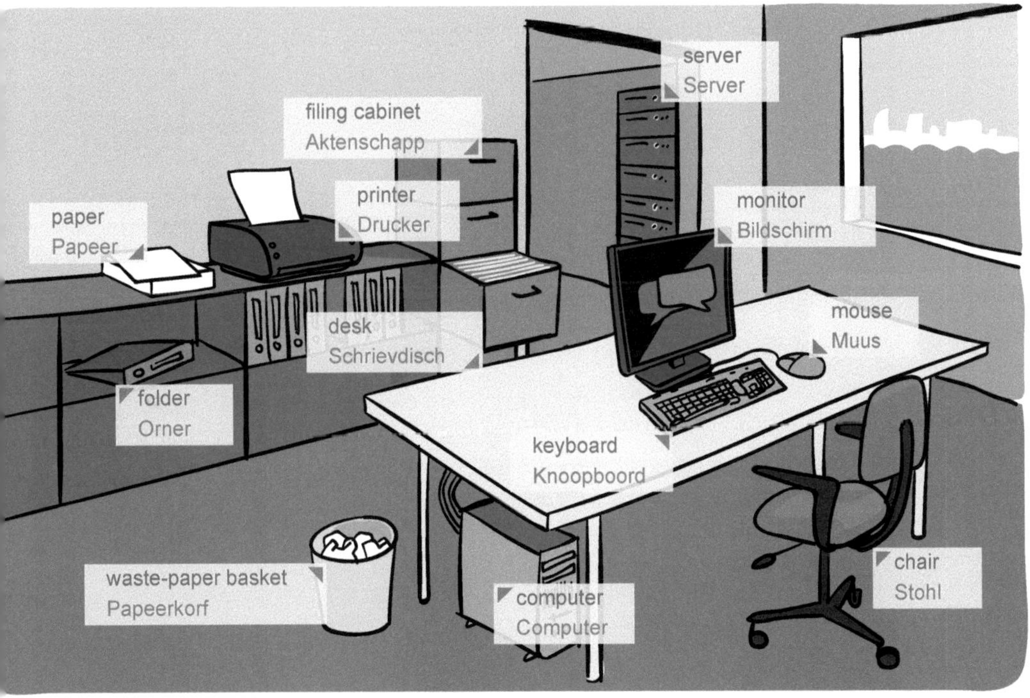

filing cabinet
Aktenschapp

server
Server

printer
Drucker

monitor
Bildschirm

paper
Papeer

mouse
Muus

desk
Schrievdisch

folder
Orner

keyboard
Knoopboord

waste-paper basket
Papeerkorf

chair
Stohl

computer
Computer

coffee mug

Koffiebeker

calculator

Taschenreekner

internet

Internet

laptop

Klappreekner

letter

Breef

message

Naricht

mobile

Ackersnacker

network

Nettwark

photocopier

Kopeerapparat

software

Software

telephone

Klöönkassen

plug socket

Steekdoos

fax machine

Faxapparat

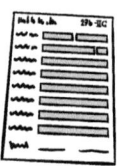

form

Formulor

document

Dokument

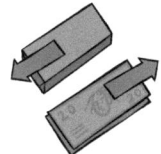

buy

köpen

pay

betahlen

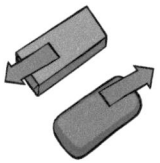

trade

hanneln

money

Geld

dollar

Dollar

euro

Euro

yen

Yen

rouble

Ruvel

Swiss franc

Swiezer Franken

renminbi yuan

Renminbi Yuan

rupee

Rupie

cashpoint

Geldautomat

bureau de change

Wesselstuuv

gold

Gold

silver

Sülver

oil

Ööl

energy

Energie

price

Pries

contract

Verdrag

tax

Stüer

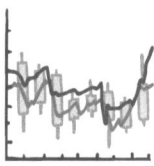

stock

Andeelschien

work

arbeiden

employee

Anstellte

employer

Arbeitgever

factory

Fabrik

shop

Hökerie

occupations
Profeschonen

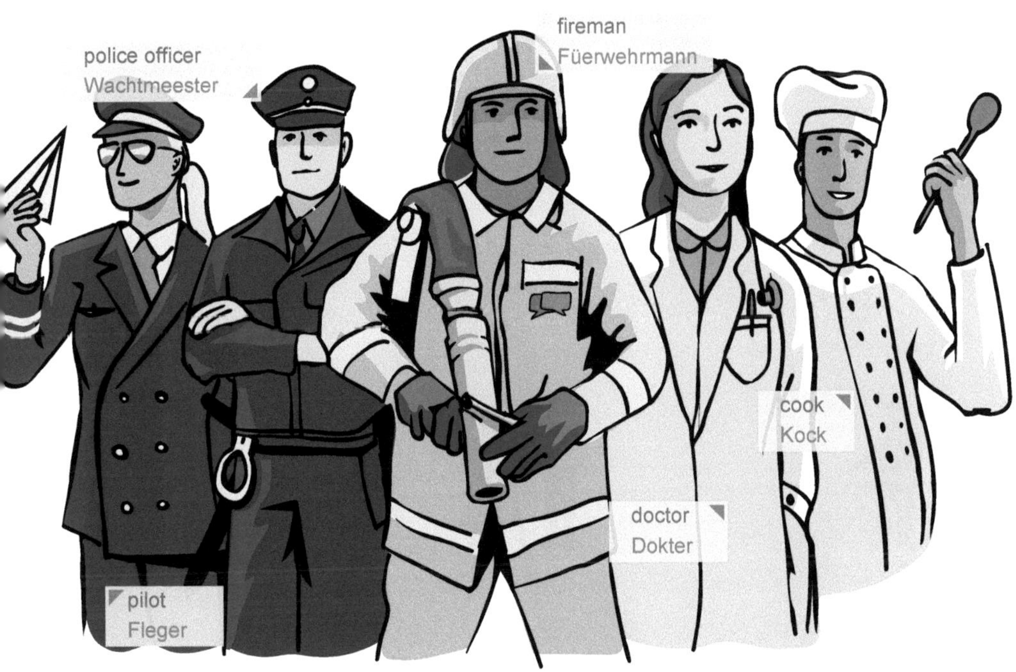
fireman
Füerwehrmann
police officer
Wachtmeester
cook
Kock
doctor
Dokter
pilot
Fleger

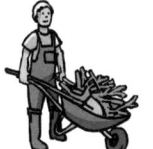

gardener

Goorner

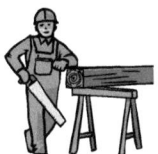

carpenter

Discher

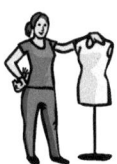

seamstress

Neihersche

judge

Richter

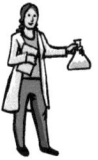

chemist

Chemiker

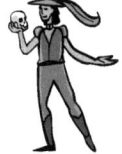

actor

Schauspeler

bus driver

Busfohrer

taxi driver

Taxifohrer

fisherman

Fischer

cleaning lady

Reinmaakfru

roofer

Dackdecker

waiter

Kellner

hunter

Jäger

painter

Maler

baker

Bäcker

electrician

Elektriker

builder

Buarbeider

engineer

Ingenieur

butcher

Slachter

plumber

Klempner

postman

Postbüdel

soldier

Suldat

architect

Architekt

cashier

Kasserer

florist

Florist

hairdresser

Putzbüdel

conductor

Schaffner

mechanic

Mechaniker

captain

Kaptein

dentist

Tähndokter

scientist

Wetenschopler

rabbi

Rabbi

imam

Imam

monk

Mönk

clergyman

Paap

tools
Warktüüch

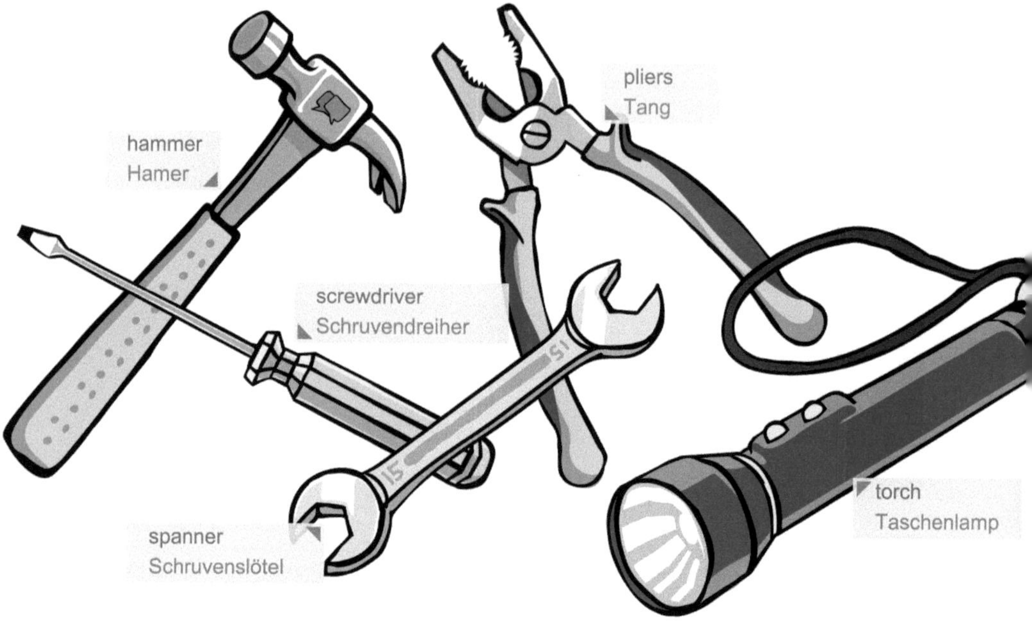
hammer
Hamer
pliers
Tang
screwdriver
Schruvendreiher
spanner
Schruvenslötel
torch
Taschenlamp

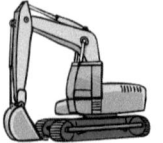

digger

Grieper

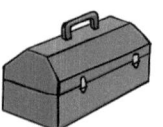

toolbox

Warktüüchkassen

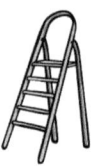

ladder

Ledder

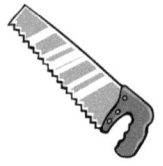

saw

Saag

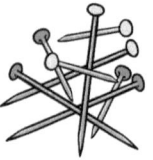

nails

Nagels

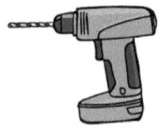

drill

Bohrer

repair
....
heelmaken

shovel
....
Schüffel

Damn!
....
Schiet!

dustpan
....
Kehrblick

paint pot
....
Farvpott

screws
....
Schruven

musical instruments
Musikinstrumenten

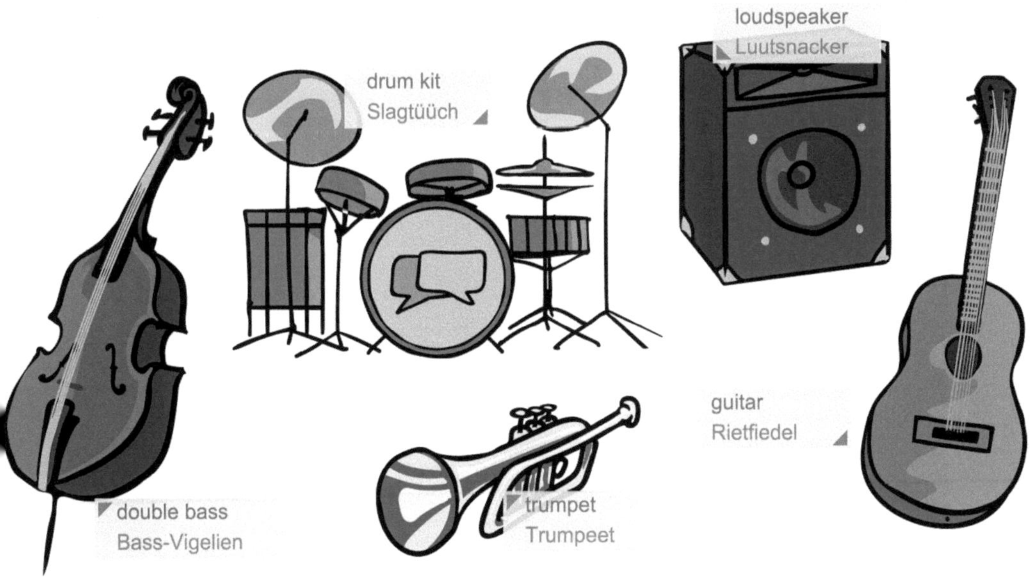

loudspeaker
Luutsnacker

drum kit
Slagtüüch

guitar
Rietfiedel

double bass
Bass-Vigelien

trumpet
Trumpeet

piano

Klaveer

violin

Vigelien

bass

Bass

timpani

Pauk

drums

Trummeln

keyboard

Keyboard

saxophone

Saxophon

flute

Fleut

microphone

Mikrofoon

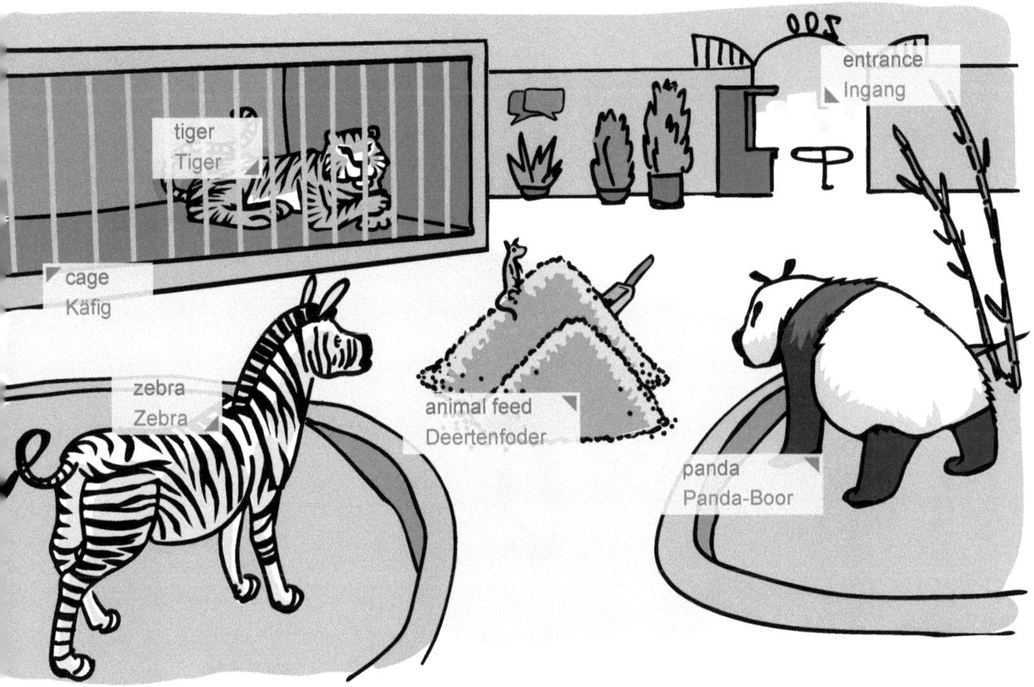

tiger
Tiger

entrance
Ingang

cage
Käfig

zebra
Zebra

animal feed
Deertenfoder

panda
Panda-Boor

animals

Deerten

elephant

Elefant

kangaroo

Känguru

rhino

Neeshoorn

gorilla

Gorilla

bear

Boor

camel

Kameel

ostrich

Struuß

lion

Lööv

monkey

Aap

flamingo

Flamingo

parrot

Papagoi

polar bear

Iesboor

penguin

Pinguin

shark

Haifisch

peacock

Pageluun

snake

Slang

crocodile

Krokodil

zookeeper

Oppasser in'n Deertenpark

seal

Saalhund

jaguar

Jaguor

pony
Pony

leopard
Leopard

hippo
Nilpeerd

giraffe
Giraff

eagle
Aadler

boar
Wildswien

fish
Fisch

turtle
Schildkrööt

walrus
Walross

fox
Voss

gazelle
Gazell

American football
Amerikaansch Football

cycling
Radfohren

tennis
Tennis

basketball
Korfball

swimming
Swümmen

ice hockey
Ieshockey

boxing
Boxen

football
Football

badminton
Fedderball

athletics
Leichtathletik

handball
Handball

skiing
Skilopen

polo
Polo

activities
Aktivitäten

jump
springen
hug
ümarmen
laugh
lachen
walk
gahn
sing
singen
dream
drömen
pray
beden
kiss
snuteln

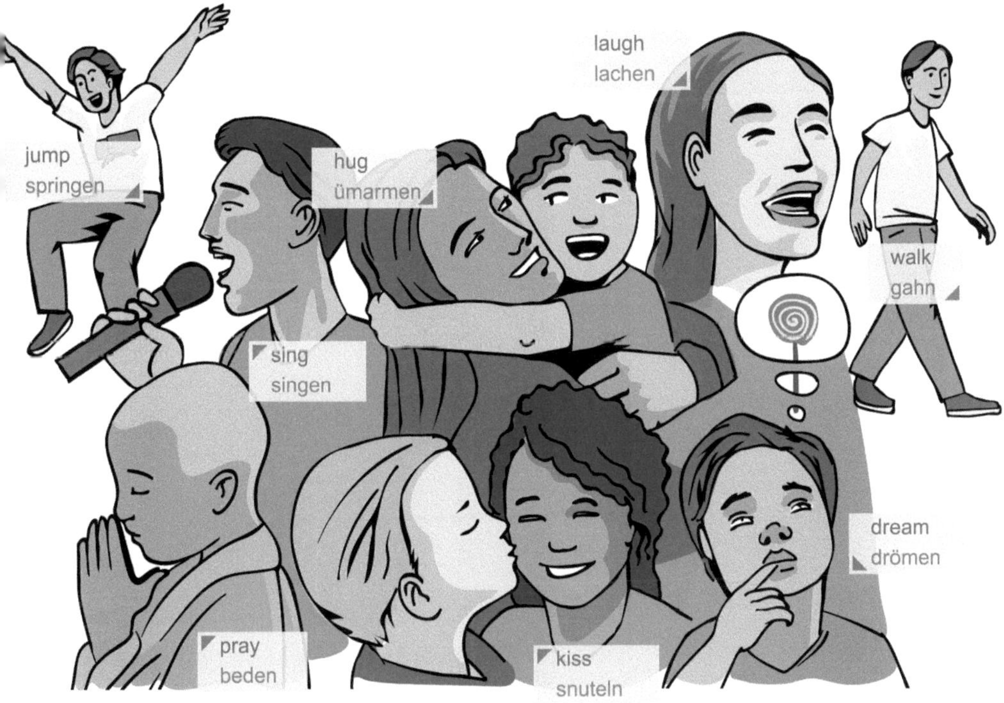

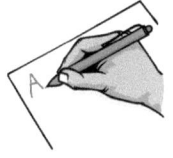

write

schrieven

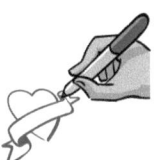

draw

teken

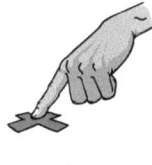

show

wiesen

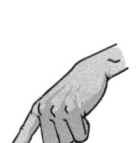

push

drücken

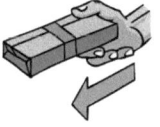

give

geven

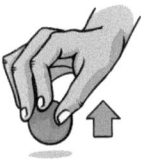

take

nehmen

have

hebben

do

doon

be

sien

stand

stahn

run

lopen

pull

trecken

throw

smieten

fall

fallen

lie

liggen

wait

töven

carry

dregen

sit

sitten

get dressed

antrecken

sleep

slapen

wake up

opwaken

look at

ankieken

cry

wenen

stroke

eien

comb

kämmen

talk

snacken

understand

verstahn

ask

fragen

listen

hören

drink

drinken

eat

eten

tidy up

oprümen

love

leefhebben

cook

kaken

drive

fohren

fly

flegen

sail

segeln

calculate

reken

read

lesen

learn

lehren

work

arbeiden

marry

de Plünnen tohoopsmieten

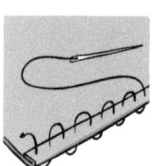

sew

neihen

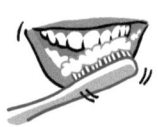

brush teeth

Tähnen putzen

kill

dootmaken

smoke

smöken

send

schicken

family
Familje

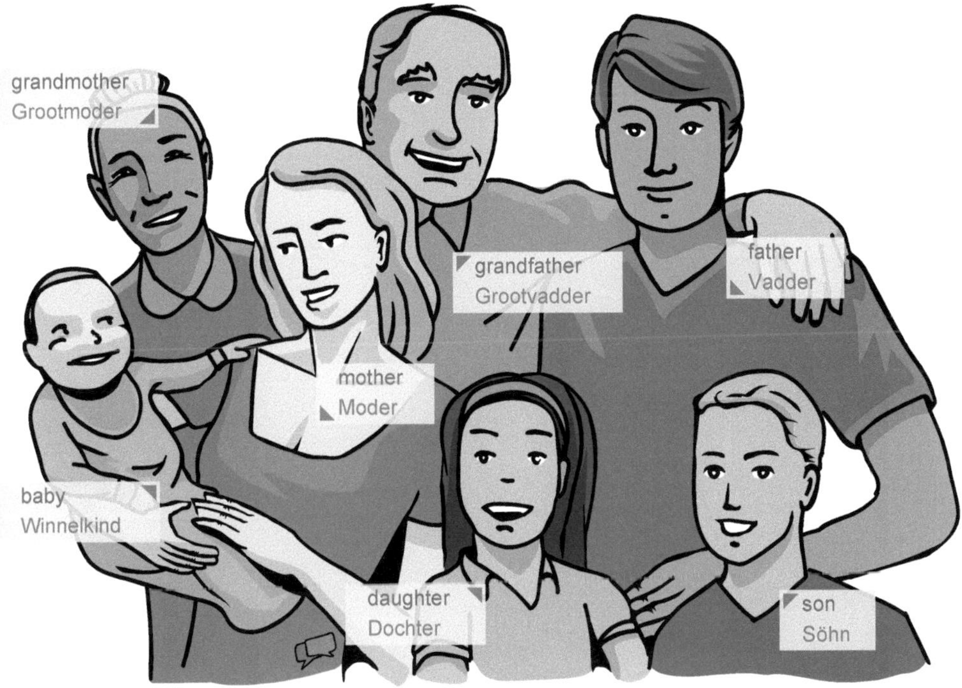
grandmother
Grootmoder
grandfather
Grootvadder
father
Vadder
mother
Moder
baby
Winnelkind
daughter
Dochter
son
Söhn

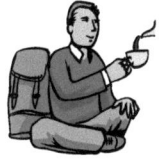

guest
Gast

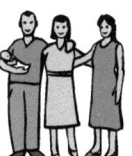

aunt
Tant

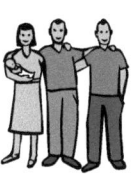

uncle
Unkel

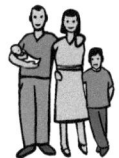

brother
Broder

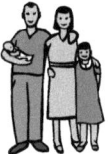

sister
Süster

body

Lief

forehead
Vörkopp
eye
Oog
shoulder
Schuller
finger
Finger
face
Gesicht
chin
Kinn
hand
Hand
leg
Been
breast
Bost
arm
Arm

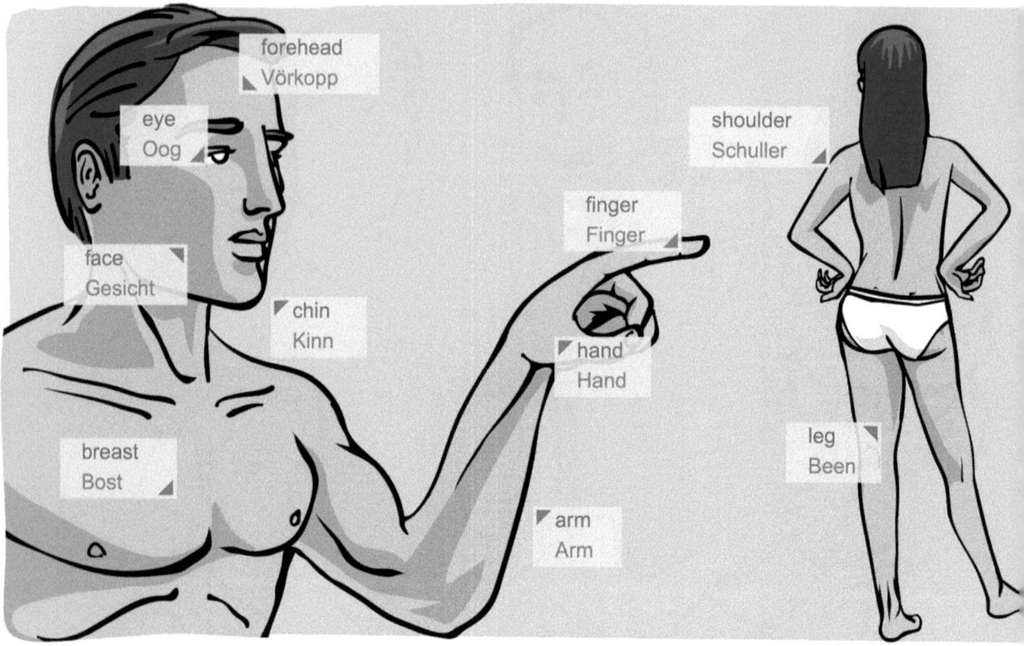

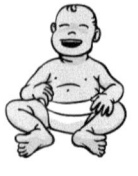

baby

Winnelkind

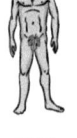

man

Mann

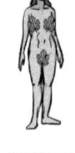

woman

Fro

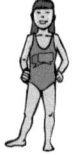

girl

Deern

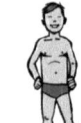

boy

Jung

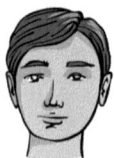

head

Arm

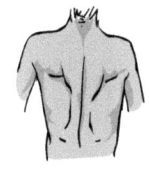

back
Rüch

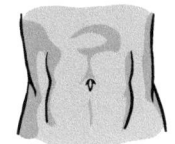

belly
Buuk

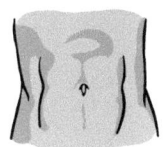

belly button
Navel

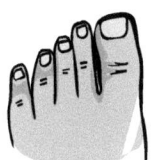

toe
Teh

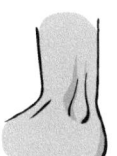

heel
Hack

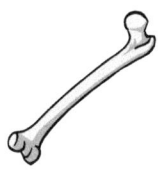

bone
Knaken

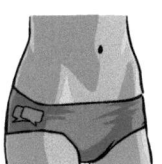

hip
Hüft

knee
Knee

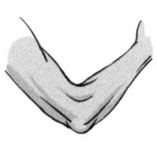

elbow
Ellbagen

nose
Nees

bottom
Achtersen

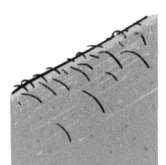

skin
Huut

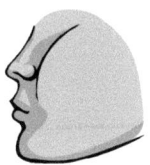

cheek
Back

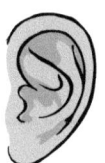

ear
Ohr

lip
Lipp

mouth

Mund

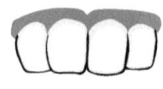

tooth

Tähn

tongue

Tung

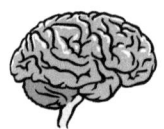

brain

Bregen

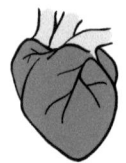

heart

Hart

muscle

Muskel

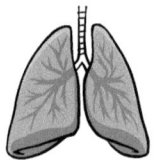

lung

Lung

liver

Lever

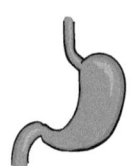

stomach

Maag

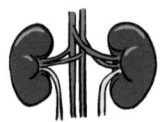

kidneys

Neren

sex

Bislaap

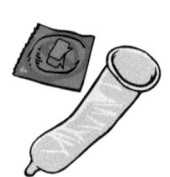

condom

Kondoom

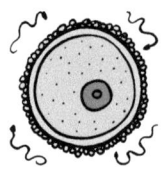

ovum

Eizell

semen

Sperma

pregnancy

Anner Ümstänn

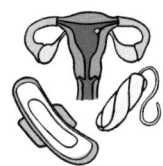

menstruation
Menstruatschoon

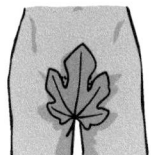

vagina
Scheed

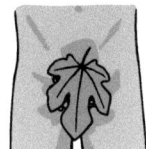

penis
Pint

eyebrow
Ogenbroe

hair
Hoor

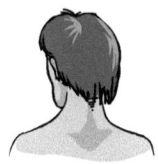

neck
Hals

hospital
Krankenhuus

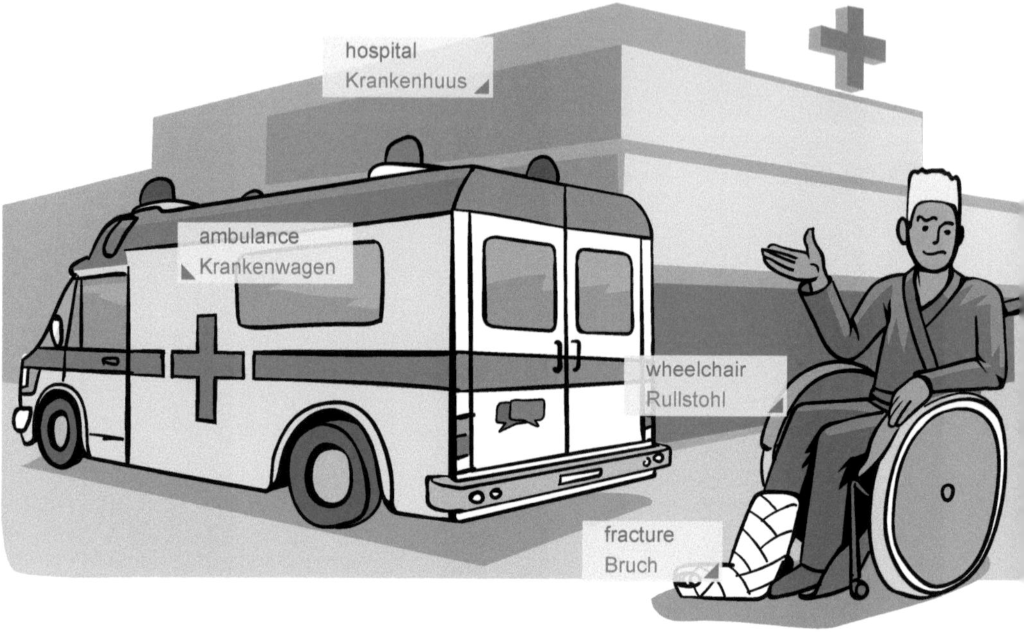

hospital
Krankenhuus
ambulance
Krankenwagen
wheelchair
Rullstohl
fracture
Bruch

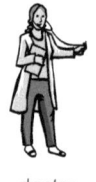

doctor
Dokter

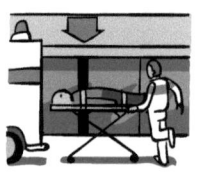

emergency room
Nootopnahm

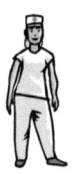

nurse
Krankensüster

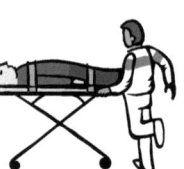

emergency
Nootfall

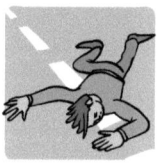

unconscious
ahnmächtig

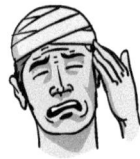

pain
Wehdaag

injury

Verwunnen

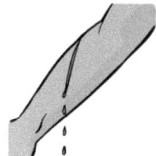

bleeding

Blöden

heart attack

Hartinfarkt

stroke

Slaganfall

allergy

Allergie

cough

Hoosten

fever

Fever

flu

Gripp

diarrhoea

Dörchfall

headache

Koppwehdaag

cancer

Kreeft

diabetes

Zuckersüük

surgeon

Chirurg

scalpel

Chirurgsch Mess

operation

Operatschoon

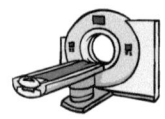

CT
CT

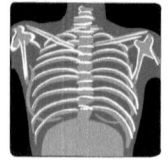

x-ray
Dörchlüchten

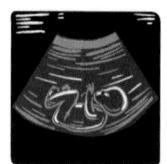

ultrasound
Ultraschall

face mask
Mask

disease
Krankheit

waiting room
Töövruum

crutch
Krück

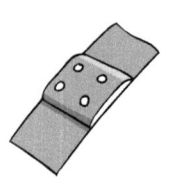

plaster
Plaaster

bandage
Verband

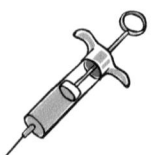

injection
Insprütten

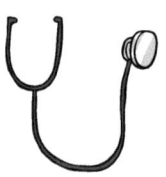

stethoscope
Stethoskop

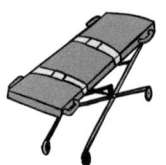

stretcher
Draag

clinical thermometer
Feverthermometer

birth
Geboort

overweight
Övergewicht

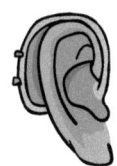

hearing aid

Höörapparat

disinfectant

Kiemfriemiddel

infection

Ansteken

virus

Virus

HIV / AIDS

HIV / AIDS

medicine

Heelmiddel

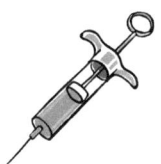

vaccination

Impen

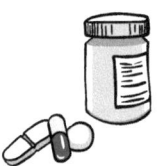

tablets

Tabletten

pill

Pill

emergency call

Nootroop

blood pressure monitor

Blootdruck-Meter

ill / healthy

krank / gesund

alarm

Alarm

assault

Överfall

Help!

Hölp!

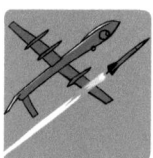

attack

Angreep

danger

Gefohr

emergency exit

Nootutgang

Fire!

Füer!

fire extinguisher

Füerlöscher

accident

Unfall

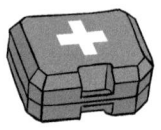

first-aid kit

Noothölpkoffer

SOS

SOS

police

Polizei

Europe

Europa

North America

Noordamerika

South America

Süüdamerika

Africa

Afrika

Asia

Asien

Australia

Australien

Atlantic

Atlantik

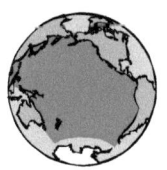

Pacific

Pazifik

Indian Ocean

Indisch Weltmeer

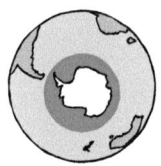

Antarctic Ocean

Antarktisch Weltmeer

Arctic Ocean

Arktisch Weltmeer

North Pole

Noordpol

South Pole
Süüdpol

Antarctica
Antarktis

Earth
Eerd

land
Land

sea
See

island
Eiland

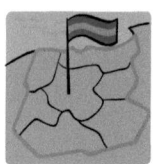

nation
Natschoon

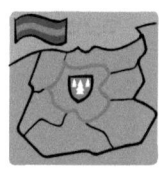

state
Staat

clock face

Tallenblatt

hour hand

Stunnenwieser

minute hand

Minutenwieser

second hand

Sekunnenwieser

What time is it?

Wo laat is dat?

day

Dag

time

Tiet

now

nu

digital watch

digetaalsch Klock

minute

Minuut

hour

Stunn

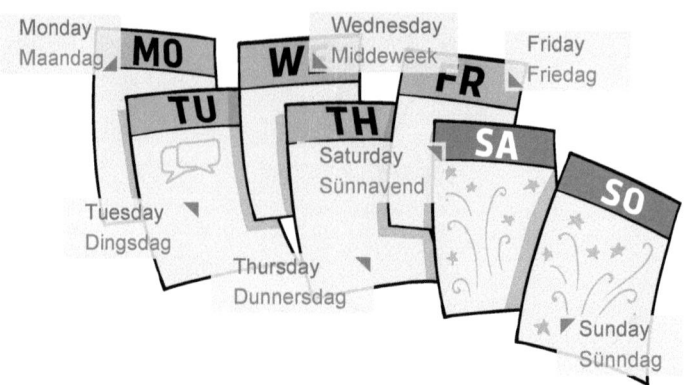

Monday
Maandag
MO

W
Wednesday
Middeweek

Friday
Friedag
FR

TU

TH

SA

SO

Tuesday
Dingsdag

Saturday
Sünnavend

Thursday
Dunnersdag

Sunday
Sünndag

yesterday

güstern

today

hüüt

tomorrow

morgen

morning

Morgen

noon

Meddag

evening

Avend

business days

Arbeitsdaag

weekend

Wekenenn

year
Johr

rain
Regen
spring
Fröhjohr
summer
Sommer
wind
Wind
autumn
Harvst
snow
Snee
winter
Winter

4.APRIL 11°
5.APRIL 4°
6.APRIL 13°
7.APRIL 8°
8.APRIL 10°

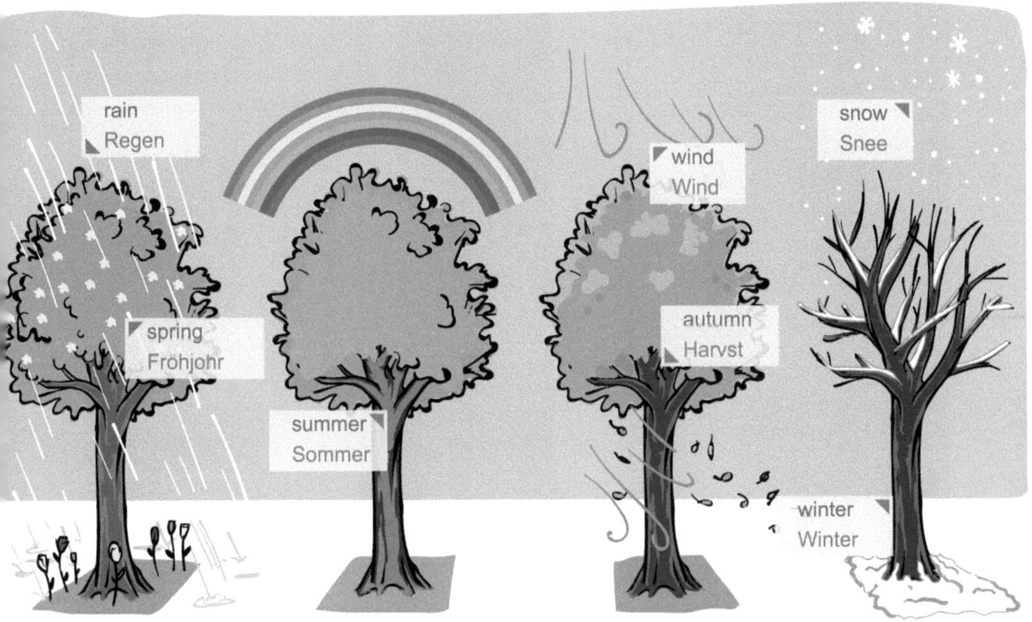

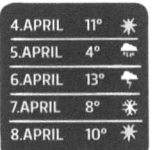

weather forecast

Wedervörhersaag

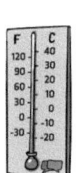

thermometer

Thermometer

sunshine

Sünnenschien

cloud

Wulk

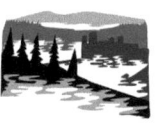

fog

Nevel

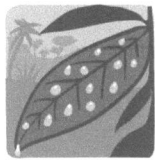

humidity

Luftfuchtigkeit

lightning

Blitz

thunder

Dunner

storm

Storm

hail

Hagel

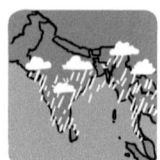

monsoon

Monsun

flood

Floot

ice

Ies

January

Januormaand

February

Februormaand

March

Martmaand

April

Aprilmaand

May

Maimaand

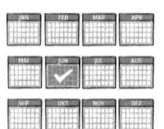

June

Junimaand

July

Julimaand

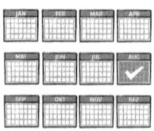

August

Augustmaand

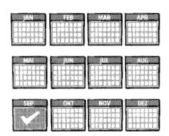

September

Septembermaand

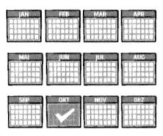

October

Oktobermaand

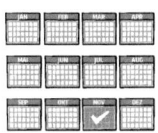

November

Novembermaand

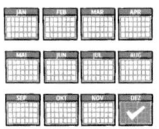

December

Dezembermaand

shapes

Formen

circle

Krink

square

Quadrat

rectangle

Rechteck

triangle

Dreeeck

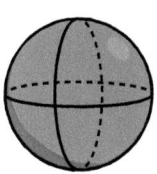

sphere

Kugel

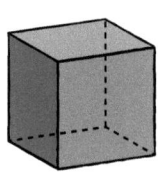

cube

Wörpel

white

witt

yellow

geel

orange

orangsch

pink

pink

red

root

purple

lila

blue

blau

green

gröön

brown

bruun

grey

gries

black

swart

a lot / a little

veel / wenig

angry / calm

böös / verdreeglich

beautiful / ugly

smuck / mies

beginning / end

Begünn / Enn

big / small

groot / lütt

bright / dark

hell / düüster

brother / sister

Broder / Süster

clean / dirty

schier / schietig

complete / incomplete

kumpleet / nich kumpleet

day / night

Dag / Nacht

dead / alive

doot / lebennig

wide / narrow

breet / small

edible / inedible

geneetbor / nich geneetbor

evil / kind

böös / fründlich

excited / bored

fickerig / langwielt

fat / thin

dick / dünn

first / last

toeerst / toletzt

friend / enemy

Fründ / Fiend

full / empty

vull / leddig

hard / soft

hart / week

heavy / light

swoor / licht

hunger / thirst

Smacht / Döst

ill / healthy

krank / gesund

illegal / legal

nich na't Recht / na't Recht

intelligent / stupid

klook / dummerhaftig

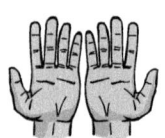

left / right

linkerhand / rechterhand

near / far

neeg / feern

new / used

nieg / bruukt

nothing / something

nix / wat

old / young

oolt / jung

on / off

an / ut

open / closed

apen / slaten

quiet / loud

lies / luut

rich / poor

riek / arm

right / wrong

richtig / verkehrt

rough / smooth

ruug / glatt

sad / happy

trurig / glücklich

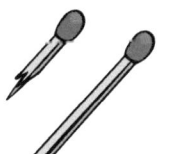

short / long

kort / lang

slow / fast

suutje / flink

wet / dry

natt / dröög

warm / cool

warm / köhl

war / peace

Krieg / Freden

0

zero

null

1

one

een

2

two

twee

3

three

dree

4

four

veer

5

five

fief

6

six

söss

7

seven

söven

8

eight

acht

9

nine

negen

10

ten

teihn

11

eleven

ölven

12

twelve
twölf

13

thirteen
dörteihn

14

fourteen
veerteihn

15

fifteen
föffteihn

16

sixteen
sössteihn

17

seventeen
söventeihn

18

eighteen
achtteihn

19

nineteen
negenteihn

20

twenty
twintig

100

hundred
hunnert

1.000

thousand
dusend

1.000.000

million
million

English

Engelsch

American English

Amerikaansch Engelsch

Chinese Mandarin

Chineesch Mandarin

Hindi

Hindi

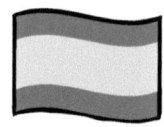

Spanish

Spaansch

French

Franzöösch

Arabic

Araabsch

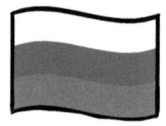

Russian

Rusch

Portuguese

Portugiesch

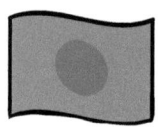

Bengali

Bengaalsch

German

Düütsch

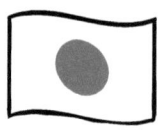

Japanese

Japaansch

I

ik

you

du

he / she / it

he / se / dat

we

wi

you

ji

they

se

who?

keen?

what?

wat?

how?

woans?

where?

woneem?

when?

wannehr?

name

Naam

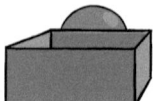

behind

achter

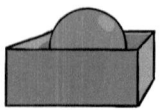

in

in

in front of

vör

over

över

on

op

under

ünner

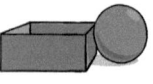

beside

blangen

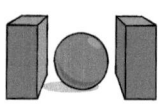

between

twüschen

place

Oort